YEAR OF THE RAT

To Malcolm & Ang for their glorious support

Roy Smiles

YEAR OF THE RAT

'We are all serving a life sentence in the dungeon of self.'
CYRIL CONNOLLY

OBERON BOOKS
LONDON

First published in 2008 by Oberon Books Ltd
521 Caledonian Road, London N7 9RH
Tel: 020 7607 3637 / Fax: 020 7607 3629
e-mail: info@oberonbooks.com
www.oberonbooks.com

A catalogue record for this book is available from the British
Library.

ISBN: 978-1-84002-844-7

Cover image by West Yorkshire Playhouse

Printed in Great Britain by Antony Rowe Ltd, Chippenham

Characters

GEORGE ORWELL – a writer

SONIA BROWNELL – his wife-to-be

CYRIL CONNOLLY – his friend

BOXER*

PIG*

RAT*

* These parts should be played by the
same actor.

THE SETTING
A farmhouse on the Scottish island of Jura, 1948.

WY PLAY HOUSE

The first UK performance of *Year of the Rat* was in the Courtyard Theatre, West Yorkshire Playhouse, on 7 March 2008, with the following cast:

GEORGE ORWELL, Hugo Speer

SONIA BROWNELL, Claudia Elmhirst

CYRIL CONNOLLY, Nicholas Blane

BOXER / PIG / RAT, Paul Kemp

Director Alan Strachan

Designer Michael Pavelka

Lighting Jason Taylor

Sound Mic Pool

Movement Lucinda Hind

Assistant Director Kathryn Ind

Roy Smiles would like to thank:
Terry Johnson (as per), Claire Starck, Michael Codron,
West Yorkshire Playhouse and James Clyde, Lorna Bennett,
Ben Blythe, Martin Trent and the King's Head, Islington
(for the reading).

Act One

Darkness; in the darkness a grandfather clock strikes thirteen times, in reference to the opening sentence of Nineteen Eighty-Four.

As the sound of the striking clock fades the sound of rain is heard. Lights rise on the ground floor of GEORGE ORWELL's rented farmhouse on the Scottish island of Jura, the Inner Hebrides, some time in 1948.

It is early evening, the light outside beginning to fade on an autumn day.

ORWELL sits at a table typing on a black, upright typewriter; an almost completed manuscript stacked before him. He is in the second-last year of his life. The lung disease that will claim him is etched in the sunken cheeks and stretched skin of his face. He wears a shabby tweed suit, a grey shirt and an ill-knotted tie.

There is a window to the left of the table where ORWELL works. Several armchairs sit in the centre of the room; an open coal fire flickers behind them.

A doorway leads to a kitchen left, another door (rear and centre) leads to a staircase and the upstairs of the farmhouse; a third door – leading to the outside – is situated far right.

A beat, then SONIA BROWNELL enters through the doorway to the stairs. She is wearing a man's dressing gown, too large for her.

She is a strong-willed and extremely good-looking woman of almost thirty: beautiful in an English rose, middle-class kind of way.

SONIA: (*Pulling at cord of dressing gown.*) I borrowed this.

ORWELL: Very fetching.

SONIA: Hardly.

ORWELL: Was the water hot?

SONIA: Not very.

ORWELL: Sorry.

SONIA: I can rough it occasionally.

ORWELL: Really?

SONIA: Don't sound so surprised.

ORWELL: I took you for the cosmopolitan type: all cocktails and triangular sandwiches.

SONIA: If you can survive convent school you can survive anything.

ORWELL: Drink?

SONIA: I thought you'd never ask.

ORWELL crosses and opens a cupboard; takes out a bottle of Scotch and some glasses.

ORWELL: I am glad you've come.

SONIA: You've invited me enough times.

ORWELL: I bored you into submission.

SONIA: No, it's good to get away.

ORWELL: Is it?

SONIA: London does get claustrophobic.

ORWELL: It's a city of seven million people, Sonia.

SONIA: And most of them end up in the *Horizon* office.

ORWELL pours and hands her a large drink; then pours himself one.

ORWELL: Is Cyril still misbehaving?

SONIA: When he's there; they do resent me, you know.

ORWELL: Who?

SONIA: The contributors; having to take editorial notes from a woman, they're misogynist bastards to a man.

ORWELL: Including me?

SONIA: You have your moments.

ORWELL: Ah.

SONIA: But at least you don't lech.

ORWELL: Don't I?

SONIA gives him a look.

SONIA: How's the novel?

ORWELL: Almost finished.

SONIA: Really?

ORWELL: Yes. I was hoping you'd read it, while you were here.

SONIA: I'd like that.

ORWELL: There's rather a reason. Not just because I value your opinion.

SONIA: What's that?

ORWELL: Well, it's just the girl in the book is, well, based on you.

SONIA: She's a total bitch is she?

ORWELL: No, strong-willed, independent – you'll like her.

SONIA: I hope so.

ORWELL: I should warn you: it's pretty bleak.

SONIA: All your books are bleak, George.

ORWELL: I can't write any other way.

SONIA: No. (*Beat.*) I can't think of anything better than writing books.

ORWELL: Really? I always fancied myself as a music-hall turn; sawing floozies in half and that sort of thing.

SONIA laughs.

Cyril says you find English literature inferior to French.

SONIA: Cyril talks out of his bottom most days. I find speaking French liberating is all.

ORWELL: From what?

SONIA: My past: Sacred Heart, India, being middle-class and all that.

ORWELL: I'm surprised he let you come.

SONIA: Actually he was insanely against the idea, to the point of tantrums.

ORWELL: Why?

SONIA: I think he thought you planned to jump me.

ORWELL: You do have a ghastly turn of phrase, Sonia.

SONIA: Well, do you?

ORWELL: What?

SONIA: Plan to jump me?

ORWELL: I might. (*Beat.*) Would I have a chance?

SONIA: What do you think?

ORWELL: I don't know. You're famously elusive.

SONIA: I refuse to sleep with the contributors, you mean.

ORWELL: I meant no offence.

SONIA: I'm tired of being called frigid by half of literary London, just because I won't succumb to their leering advances.

ORWELL: I'm making a mess of all this, sorry.

SONIA: Stop saying sorry. It's the English disease. I came didn't I?

ORWELL: Another drink?

SONIA: Are you trying to get me drunk, George?

ORWELL: With this face – it's my only option.

ORWELL pours Scotch into her glass and his.

SONIA: Eileen married you. She was a good-looking girl.

ORWELL: But not in your league.

SONIA: Do you miss her?

ORWELL: All the time.

SONIA: Cyril was very fond of her, you know.

ORWELL: Cyril is fond of anything in a skirt, save a Scotsman.

SONIA: What's the novel about, another allegory?

ORWELL: A man and a woman trying to find love in a loveless world.

SONIA: A romance?

ORWELL: Sort of.

SONIA: How unlike you.

ORWELL: I can write about other things than aspidistras.

SONIA: Am I pretty, in the novel?

ORWELL: Very.

SONIA: What's my name?

ORWELL: Julia.

SONIA: That's a lovely name.

ORWELL: Is it?

SONIA: Yes.

> *ORWELL stares. SONIA stares back. She finishes her drink with a gulp.*

Well, what shall we do now?

ORWELL: Cards?

SONIA: We could fuck.

ORWELL: Excuse me?

SONIA: It's Anglo-Saxon slang, suggesting sexual intercourse.

ORWELL: So it is.

SONIA: Isn't that the reason you asked me here?

ORWELL: Eh – one of the reasons, yes.

SONIA: You're not very good at this seduction lark are you, George?

ORWELL: Pretty rotten.

SONIA: I'd better take you in hand.

ORWELL: Very wise.

SONIA: But it will only be a bit of fun, you know that don't you?

ORWELL: Oh, of course.

SONIA: I'm not ready for another relationship.

ORWELL: Quite.

SONIA: Not after the last disaster anyway.

ORWELL: I can do fun. I haven't had much of that since Eileen died.

SONIA: Well, I should cheer you up, shouldn't I?

SONIA leans over and kisses him gently on the lips. He responds. They break off.

He stares at her awkwardly.

ORWELL: I want you to know, Sonia, that I respect you hugely.

SONIA: I don't care.

ORWELL: I'm sorry?

SONIA: I don't care if you respect me or not.

ORWELL: Shouldn't you?

SONIA: Life's too short, George.

ORWELL: You are a surprising woman, Sonia.

SONIA: That's why you like me.

ORWELL: Amongst other things.

SONIA: Was that the great Mr Orwell being smutty?

ORWELL: I do suspect it was.

SONIA: At last.

ORWELL: Do you mind if I kiss you back?

SONIA: I insist upon it.

ORWELL kisses her. They break off.

You're getting better at this.

ORWELL: Thank God.

SONIA: So – shall we do it?

ORWELL: What, here?

SONIA: (*Sighs.*) In the bedroom, George.

ORWELL: Right, right.

SONIA: We'd better go upstairs before you die of embarrassment.

ORWELL: Yes. Shall I bring the bottle?

SONIA: If you need Dutch courage.

ORWELL: Absolutely.

SONIA slips off the dressing gown as she exits up the stairs, glancing over her shoulder coquettishly, she laughs and disappears into the dark.

ORWELL polishes off his drink in one; picks up the bottle of Scotch and hurries after her, almost tripping up the stairs in his enthusiasm, he exits up the stairs.

A snap blackout; music plays – an instrumental version of: 'Poor Little Rich Girl.'

Lights rise, the next day, it is early afternoon; the room is deserted. The window is open.

After a moment ORWELL enters through the front door, carrying a shotgun; he closes the door and puts the shotgun down behind it.

The music fades.

After a long beat a horse's head appears through the window frame; this is BOXER.

BOXER: Hello George.

ORWELL: Hello Boxer.

BOXER: Where have you been?

ORWELL: Hunting rabbits.

BOXER: Did you catch any?

ORWELL: No, the little sods kept ducking.

BOXER: Where were you last night, George?

ORWELL: Shangri-La.

BOXER: Is that a good place, George?

ORWELL: It was last night.

BOXER: With that lady?

ORWELL: Last night she was no lady, thankfully.

BOXER: Is she good enough for you, George?

ORWELL: Oh, I should think so.

ORWELL sits at the desk and stares at the page in the typewriter.

BOXER: What are you writing, George?

ORWELL: A book, Boxer: a novel.

BOXER: Is it about a farm, George?

ORWELL: No: a totalitarian state.

BOXER: I thought our book was about a totalitarian state, George.

ORWELL: Call me a one-trick pony.

BOXER: But you're not a pony, George.

ORWELL: A clapped out pit pony; ready for the knacker's yard.

BOXER: I ended up in the knacker's yard, didn't I, George?

ORWELL: That's right, Boxer.

BOXER: My lungs did for me. Just like yours.

ORWELL: No, it was pigs did for you. You were loyal too long.

BOXER: I worked as hard as I could.

ORWELL: No one could have worked harder.

BOXER: You work too hard, George.

ORWELL: I've a book to finish and not much time.

BOXER: Where are you going, George?

ORWELL: Nowhere yet, not to worry.

BOXER: (*Beat.*) I don't like her, George.

ORWELL: You don't know her, Boxer.

BOXER: She'll hurt you, George.

ORWELL: Hush now.

There is the sound of footsteps coming from outside.

BOXER: Someone's coming.

ORWELL: Let them come.

BOXER: It might be – them.

ORWELL: No, they won't come for me in daylight. They haven't the guts for that. You'd better go now. My visitor might think you odd.

BOXER: Am I odd?

ORWELL: You're a talking horse.

BOXER: Be careful, George. People are dangerous.

ORWELL: I know, Boxer. I know.

BOXER disappears back through the open window.

After a beat CYRIL CONNOLLY enters through the front door, the rotund literary critic and childhood friend of ORWELL's.

He is wearing – for the climate – a patently impractical white suit, as soaked as the floppy bow tie that hangs limply from his collar. A sodden cigarette hangs from his lip.

CONNOLLY: George, George, George.

ORWELL looks up surprised.

Eric, Eric, Eric.

ORWELL continues to stare.

Have you lost the power of speech, George?

ORWELL: Hello Cyril, what are you doing here?

CONNOLLY: I just happened to be passing.

ORWELL: You live in London. This is a Scottish island.

CONNOLLY: The Inner Hebrides, how typical of you not to live in the Outer Hebrides, George, you're as introverted as ever.

ORWELL: Am I?

CONNOLLY: If you were a tube service you would be the Circle Line: cautious and self-contained. Rather than the District Line: running all over the East End like a debauched Cossack.

ORWELL: You have a nerve coming here.

CONNOLLY: Why so?

ORWELL: Last time we met socially you groped my sister.

CONNOLLY: On the contrary: I goosed her.

ORWELL: What's the difference?

CONNOLLY: Groping is so very much beneath me somehow.

ORWELL: It was beneath her.

CONNOLLY: I do apologise. I mistook her bottom for a personal friend. It was the wine, or rather, the excess of it.

ORWELL: You're incorrigible.

CONNOLLY: Naturally.

ORWELL: You're also wet.

CONNOLLY: I've been wet since Eton, if not before.

ORWELL: Literally.

CONNOLLY: Yes.

ORWELL: Is it raining?

CONNOLLY: It always rains in Scotland, George. They blame the English.

ORWELL: I didn't notice the rain.

CONNOLLY: You wouldn't.

ORWELL: No.

CONNOLLY: How's the health?

ORWELL: Not good. I seem to have collapsed a lung.

CONNOLLY: Careless of you.

ORWELL: Quite.

CONNOLLY: Of course in a British Isles where the population is either suffering from diarrhoea, constipation, flatulence or worse, a healthy writer is communicating with a hostile audience.

ORWELL: If you say so.

CONNOLLY: I do. Save for during holidays or religious festivals no author should ever be fitter than his public.

ORWELL: You do talk bilge, Cyril.

CONNOLLY: Indeed. I'm famous for it.

ORWELL: How did you get here?

CONNOLLY: I've come post-haste, by wagon train and canoe.

ORWELL: There's a perfectly functioning train that runs to Glasgow.

CONNOLLY: Yes, I was on it. I hired a boat from Oban. Captained by a man who looks as if he takes sexual advantage of herring – and enjoys it; thus we sailed storm-lashed seas. I thought he was speaking Gaelic for most of the journey. It was only whilst I was disembarking that I realized the drivel pouring out of his mouth was actually Glaswegian.

ORWELL: Why didn't you call?

CONNOLLY: You haven't got a telephone.

ORWELL: Why didn't you write?

CONNOLLY: I was aiming for the element of surprise.

ORWELL: Well, you achieved that.

CONNOLLY: I thought you'd be pleased to see me.

ORWELL: I am pleased to see you, in a perverse way.

CONNOLLY: Then why are you looking so miserable?

ORWELL: Apparently I have a woeful countenance.

CONNOLLY: Like an undertaker's clerk, who's been caught fiddling with the clientele.

ORWELL: That's very good. (*Beat.*) Did you get my manuscript?

CONNOLLY: Yes, I got your manuscript. (*Beat.*) You look like him.

ORWELL: Who?

CONNOLLY: Your anti-hero: Winston Smith.

ORWELL: Before or after the torture?

CONNOLLY: Guess. (*Beat.*) Where's Sonia?

ORWELL: At the shop.

CONNOLLY: Back soon?

ORWELL: She'll be a while, it's seven miles away.

CONNOLLY: And the boy?

ORWELL: With my sister: in Islington.

CONNOLLY: Good. 'There's no more sombre enemy of art than the pram in the hall.'

ORWELL: I haven't got a hall.

CONNOLLY: I never let reality interfere with a quip. (*Beat.*) And the book?

ORWELL: On the last pages.

CONNOLLY: Dear God, you work fast.

ORWELL: Another day's work, maybe two; and it should be ready for the publishers.

CONNOLLY: Ah, publishers: 'as repressed sadists are supposed to become policemen or butchers so those with an irrational fear of life become publishers'.

ORWELL: You seem to be quoting yourself, at length.

CONNOLLY: I always do. I'm my favourite writer.

ORWELL: How is your writing?

CONNOLLY: The new novel flows, like the Don.

ORWELL: What's it called?

CONNOLLY: *Failure & How To Achieve It.*

ORWELL: You're making that up.

CONNOLLY: Of course, still, it will be an improvement on *The Rock Pool*.

ORWELL: I rather liked it.

CONNOLLY: You were in a majority of one. Novels about depressed lesbians just don't seem to sell.

ORWELL: You surprise me.

CONNOLLY: I'll never amount to anything I suppose. (*Sighs.*) What is there to say about someone who did nothing with his life save sit on his flabby arse and write reviews?

ORWELL: Don't start that again.

CONNOLLY: And they shall write on my gravestone:

'At Eton with Orwell, at Oxford with Waugh,
He was nobody afterwards and nothing before.'

ORWELL: No, they won't. They'll write: 'under this sod – lies another'.

CONNOLLY: I won't pretend I don't resent your success; the green-eyed God consumes me daily. I will get even however. I'm thinking of informing the *Daily Express* that between writing best-selling novels you molest chickens.

ORWELL: It always amuses me when people assume I'm successful; my life's been overwhelmed by disappointment and failure. I expect that's why I'm in semi-retreat from the world.

CONNOLLY: Your fake humility would put Uriah Heep to shame.

ORWELL: You're something of a Dickensian figure yourself. (*Beat.*) How's London?

CONNOLLY: If the gossip doesn't kill me – the rationing might.

ORWELL: You eat too much. You always did.

CONNOLLY: Outside of self-abuse it's my only hobby.

ORWELL: Must you share that?

CONNOLLY: This body and rationing were never meant to co-exist, George. Is there a greater aberration before God than pork luncheon meat? Whenever I see a plate of spam I know that evil exists upon this earth and is indeed triumphant.

ORWELL: I'm rather fond of Woolton pie.

CONNOLLY: You've always had plebeian tastes. That's why you loved the war. It finally allowed you to be at one with the proletarian hordes.

ORWELL: It was a People's War, Cyril. It wasn't the chinless wonders and Colonel Blimps of the officer class who brought Hitler down. It was working-class young men from the slums of Gateshead and the backstreets of Slough, with their bad teeth and poor skin and rotten eyesight. They're the real heirs of Nelson and Cromwell; this is a country run by ghouls, Cyril, in their country houses and on their grouse moors. But their end is nigh; all the Tory legions and their capitalist cohorts. Those people don't believe in society. They have shadows where their souls should be.

CONNOLLY: You're pontificating again.

ORWELL: It's what I do.

CONNOLLY: Yes, I know.

CONNOLLY sits, glancing around.

This reminds me of St Cyprians, that merry little concentration camp masquerading as our preparatory school.

ORWELL: Was it that bad? Between the bed wetting and the sobbing I hardly noticed.

CONNOLLY: Almost as squalid as this; prisoners in the 'slammer' would complain about these conditions, George.

ORWELL: I suppose they might.

CONNOLLY: You're the only fellow I know who'd be perfectly happy banged up in the Bastille, living off bread, water and the occasional rat.

ORWELL: I don't need much.

CONNOLLY: And what of Sonia, does she need 'much'?

ORWELL: She's only here for the week.

CONNOLLY: Just the week?

ORWELL: Yes, just the week.

CONNOLLY: I should never have let her out of my sight of course, the office needs her.

ORWELL: Only because she does all the work.

CONNOLLY: What are assistants for?

ORWELL: Have you ever considered breaking into a sweat yourself?

CONNOLLY: Don't be ridiculous. (*Beat.*) Well, your farm book is still kicking up something of a worldwide hoo-ha.

ORWELL: It is rather.

CONNOLLY: Who'd have thought it, our Georgie famous?

ORWELL: Me least of all.

CONNOLLY: Brother Muggeridge reports from his connections in Moscow that it's irritated Uncle Joe quite tremendously.

ORWELL: Good.

CONNOLLY: Citizen Stalin rather resents being represented by a pig.

23

ORWELL: I couldn't think of anything more offensive to compare him with.

CONNOLLY: You should be careful, old son. Look what he did to Mr Trotsky whilst he was at the pictures: ice pick, back of the neck, goodbye cruel world.

ORWELL: I might suffer the same fate yet.

CONNOLLY: Death by ice pick would be the sincerest form of literary criticism.

ORWELL: Stalin's not funny, Cyril.

CONNOLLY: Unlike our own dear Prime Minister of course.

ORWELL: I support Attlee.

CONNOLLY: Despite the fact he looks like a lingerie salesman from Watford.

ORWELL: He's made a total botch of the withdrawal from India of course. And Burma, it was grim enough when I was there.

CONNOLLY: Yet so gloriously scenic betwixt the mounds of elephant dung; (*Beat.*) didn't you shoot an elephant once, George?

ORWELL: It was running amok.

CONNOLLY: Evelyn Waugh runs amok, throughout literary London. Yet they don't shoot him. If only they would. I'd buy a ticket.

ORWELL: Is he still bitching behind your back?

CONNOLLY: And to my front; still, he's not as bad as Tony 'bums away' Powell, he bitches for England.

ORWELL: Powell's the only Tory I've ever liked.

CONNOLLY: A nancy is a nancy: left wing or right.

ORWELL: I seem to recall at Eton you rather liked chasing boys yourself.

CONNOLLY: And caught them; alas, it's just women these days.

ORWELL: I notice the plural. You've taken a mistress again, haven't you? You have the moral scruples of a bullock.

CONNOLLY: Fucking women is infinitely preferable to fucking typing. I need the emotional turmoil, George. It distracts me when I can't write, which is most days. I seem to have fallen between the twin stools of perfectionism and laziness and I'm too bone idle to reach either. Living proof an Englishman's sloth is his castle.

ORWELL: Why are you actually here?

CONNOLLY: Ah, therein lies a tale.

ORWELL: So spill the beans.

CONNOLLY: Must you come out with these ghastly Americanisms?

ORWELL: It's pretty inconvenient you're here, you know, very inconvenient as a matter of fact.

CONNOLLY: Am I interrupting a moment of profound social significance?

ORWELL: Yes. You see –

CONNOLLY: Do you mind if I have a glass of water? I seem to be overwhelmed by thirst of the non-alcoholic kind. You do have running water?

ORWELL: Just.

As CONNOLLY enters the kitchen:

CONNOLLY: Is this a kitchen or where cockroaches go to die?

ORWELL: Both.

CONNOLLY exits. After a long pause a human-sized PIG lowers from the ceiling on a circus swing, representing the Soviet dictator Joseph Stalin.

PIG: Afternoon comrade.

ORWELL: Don't call me that.

PIG: Why ever not?

ORWELL: You've never been a 'comrade' to anyone in your life.

PIG: Just what have you got against me, George?

ORWELL: You've killed millions of your own people.

PIG: Ah, but they all died equal.

ORWELL: Some equality is that.

PIG: You don't think Trotsky would have slaughtered as many?

ORWELL: I've said it before until I'm sick: I'm no Trotskyite.

PIG: No, but you're a fellow non-traveller.

ORWELL: Oh, very good.

PIG: It was necessary bloodshed.

ORWELL: What was necessary about the slaughter of a generation?

PIG: There's a price to be paid for dragging Russia kicking and screaming into the twentieth century.

ORWELL: There was too much kicking and way too much screaming. Mass starvation in the Ukraine: even cannibalism.

PIG: Minor quibbles.

ORWELL: Christ, the Tsar had many faults but he never made his own population eat themselves.

PIG: So what the hell? The dead were just peasants. They bred like rabbits, (*Laughs.*) tasted like rabbit too apparently.

ORWELL: They were people. It's one world, one humanity, we're all in this together.

PIG: Balls, humanity has never been so tribal. Anyway, you're English, what's it matter to you what happens in Russia?

ORWELL: Because you have the British Left by the throat, that's what. It's my life's work to relieve that stranglehold.

PIG: But you're dying, George.

ORWELL: Everyone's dying.

PIG: Not as quickly as you, old son.

ORWELL: I've got long enough, one last book, perhaps another.

ORWELL points at manuscript on table.

This might tear down the walls of the Kremlin yet.

PIG: But the Right will claim you as one of their own.

ORWELL: I don't care.

PIG: Don't you? They'll use it to discredit socialism, the only cause you've ever truly believed in.

ORWELL: I'll take that risk.

PIG: It's a big risk, George. You might have just given them the greatest weapon they possess.

ORWELL: It's written as a warning to the Left, the Right can go hang.

PIG: If only it were that simple. Why not burn the new book, Big Brother and all? After all, *Animal Farm* has done the cause enough harm.

ORWELL: I wrote that book to show how the Russian Revolution was betrayed by the poisonous ego of a rabid megalomaniac.

PIG: *Moi?*

ORWELL: I wrote it for Andrés Nin.

PIG: Never heard of him.

ORWELL: Oh, I think you have.

PIG: I might have seen his act at the circus. Did he ride a llama?

ORWELL: He was the Catalan leader kidnapped, tortured and murdered on your orders.

PIG: The road to socialism is a bloody one.

ORWELL: Tell them in Eastern Europe they're living in a Socialist Utopia, they'll laugh in your twisted face.

PIG: Everyone's a critic.

ORWELL: If only the British Left would criticise you, they believe every line of your wretched propaganda.

PIG: At least they don't run away from life.

ORWELL: What makes you think I have?

PIG: Then why are you hiding on this shit-stained Scottish island?

ORWELL: I wanted to be alone.

PIG: No man is alone, George: the Spanish dead, your wife, the Burmese poor, every pauper you ever met on the ghastly road to Wigan Pier, you can hardly move in this room for ghosts. Alone? You're fooling yourself. If you want company you should join them. You've got a shotgun after all.

ORWELL: What about it?

PIG: Why not put it in your mouth? Suck it like a public schoolboy's dick, pull the trigger, goodnight Vienna.

ORWELL: Are you the Devil?

PIG: Close.

ORWELL: Then bugger off. I'm not ready for that yet.

PIG: Oh, but soon.

ORWELL: You'll be waiting until Kingdom Come.

PIG: Aren't we brave?

ORWELL: Brave enough.

PIG: Ah, well, must dash, its feeding time; (*Cackles.*) there's a peasant cooking slowly somewhere in the Ukraine, its pork for dinner tonight. Every pig must have his trough. (*Shouts.*) All power to the swineherds!

PIG disappears into the ceiling on his circus swing. ORWELL stares after him.

A silence then CONNOLLY re-enters, carrying a glass of dubious-looking water.

CONNOLLY: A hand-pump, just to get water; Cold Comfort Farm has nothing on this place. When does the village idiot arrive?

ORWELL: You have arrived.

CONNOLLY: Oh, very good. (*Peers at water.*) I think a haggis pissed in this.

ORWELL: Not satisfied with the service? Stay in a hotel.

CONNOLLY: There's a hotel?

ORWELL: No.

CONNOLLY: A hostel then?

ORWELL: Not to my knowledge.

CONNOLLY: Siberia would be more welcoming, George.

ORWELL: I might end up there yet.

CONNOLLY: Always the optimist; (*Beat.*) should you be here, George, really, with your chest? To catch pneumonia once is unfortunate, to catch it twice is unlucky, to catch it three times is downright perverse, to catch it four times – (*In exasperation.*) do you ever wear a vest?

ORWELL: Look, I appreciate your concern but I still need you to leave.

CONNOLLY: Leave, now?

ORWELL: Yes. Swim back to the mainland if you have to.

CONNOLLY: And be harpooned by a whaling fleet? I don't think so, George.

ORWELL: I don't want you here.

CONNOLLY: I'm not leaving. Not yet.

ORWELL: Why not?

CONNOLLY: You need me.

ORWELL: Since when?

CONNOLLY: Since I got your manuscript.

ORWELL: What about my manuscript?

CONNOLLY: It was the letter that came with it.

ORWELL: Letter?

CONNOLLY: You can't kid a kidder, George.

ORWELL: Is that gibberish masquerading as profundity or the reverse?

CONNOLLY: If you think I'm going to just stand by –

ORWELL: You seem to be speaking in tongues.

CONNOLLY: You've got to let this grotesque charade –

At this moment: SONIA enters from the outside. Carrying a large basket and an umbrella, her head covered in a headscarf; wearing boots and thick overcoat. She stops abruptly when she sees CONNOLLY.

SONIA: Oh. Hello Cyril.

CONNOLLY: Do sound more enthusiastic, Sonia.

She lowers the basket, takes off the headscarf, crosses and kisses CONNOLLY affectionately on the cheek.

SONIA: It is nice to see you. (*Beat.*) How's the office?

CONNOLLY: Without you: chaos.

SONIA: I can't believe you're out of London.

CONNOLLY: 'No city should be too large for a man to walk out of in the morning.'

SONIA: You walked here?

CONNOLLY: Like Marco Polo I packed my trunk and said farewell to the civilised world.

SONIA: What trunk? You came without a change of clothes?

CONNOLLY: I brought a toothbrush.

SONIA: Is that all? How hygienic.

CONNOLLY: A slob and his underpants are seldom parted.

SONIA begins to remove her Wellington boots and coat.

SONIA: That's verging on disgusting.

CONNOLLY: Ah, but look at you in your *Hausfrau* mufti. Wellington boots and all the rural trimmings: you've gone all Miss Marple on me, Sonia.

SONIA: I don't think so.

CONNOLLY: I'm used to you dressed to the nines, sashaying around the dance-floor of the Gargoyle Club, surrounded by your adoring legions.

ORWELL: There's more to life than dancing and nightclubs, Cyril.

CONNOLLY: There is? I'm shocked. (*Beat.*) I'm rather a nimble dancer for a man of my girth. (*Beat.*) Actually I'm the only nimble dancer for a man of my girth.

SONIA: Stop boasting. Tea?

CONNOLLY: Yes please.

SONIA: Didn't you offer him tea, George?

ORWELL: He'd have been too busy quoting himself to drink it.

SONIA: Really, George, you really are the most uncivilised –

ORWELL: Ah, but what is 'civilisation'?

SONIA: Don't start on that. We'll be here all day. And he's wet through. I'll fetch you a towel, Cyril. Do you want some whisky in the tea?

ORWELL: Is the Pope a virgin?

SONIA: (*Laughs.*) Probably.

SONIA picks up the basket and exits. CONNOLLY stares after her.

CONNOLLY: You've a treasure there, George.

ORWELL: Yes. (*Beat.*) How is Lys?

CONNOLLY: Depressed she's living with a Zeppelin balloon; we cohabitate out of fear, George.

ORWELL: What of?

CONNOLLY: Loneliness, what else?

ORWELL: I'm rather used to loneliness.

CONNOLLY: Yet you asked Sonia here.

ORWELL: Yes.

CONNOLLY: Had your wicked way with her yet?

ORWELL: We're not all you, Cyril. In the *Horizon* offices they call you the 'Dick of Death.'

CONNOLLY: Do they? That's rather good.

ORWELL: And have you had your wicked way with Sonia, Cyril?

CONNOLLY: Absolutely not: she wouldn't let me.

ORWELL: Good.

CONNOLLY: She's slept with most of literary London of course.

ORWELL: I'd rather you didn't talk about her that way.

CONNOLLY: Always the prude: never the satyr.

ORWELL: And glad of it.

CONNOLLY: I'm always rather surprised women sleep with me. Sometimes I stare at my naked body in the mirror after a bath and I'm terribly repulsed. I look like an overfed walrus, stuffed to the gills on penguin flesh, waiting for indigestion to carry him away. Said Simple Simon to the pie-man: 'Where went all the pies?' Said the pie-man to Simple Simon: 'Fat fucking Cyril got here first.'

SONIA enters with a tray of cups, a three-quarters-full bottle of Scotch, a plate of scones and a towel over her shoulder, which she passes to CONNOLLY.

SONIA: We can have some scones with the tea.

ORWELL: (*Glancing at Connolly.*) Hold the cream.

ORWELL and CONNOLLY burst out laughing.

SONIA: What's the joke?

ORWELL: Cyril's being self-loathing again.

SONIA: Well, it is a weekday.

CONNOLLY: The Humpty Dumpty of Fitzrovia and the wraith of Canonbury; what did we ever have in common, George?

ORWELL: That's easy: ugliness.

SONIA: Now who's being self-loathing?

She exits into the kitchen. CONNOLLY attempts to dry himself with the towel.

CONNOLLY: You've got the most efficient editor and most lusted-after woman in London making you tea, George. What's the secret?

ORWELL: TB.

CONNOLLY: How do you catch it again?

ORWELL: Inhale next to a badger.

CONNOLLY: (*Beat.*) She's just here for the week?

ORWELL: Yes, just the week.

CONNOLLY: She's a lesbian of course.

ORWELL: Who?

CONNOLLY: Sonia.

ORWELL: Because a woman won't sleep with you she's automatically a lesbian?

CONNOLLY: That's about the colour of my Universe, yes.

ORWELL: What an appalling misogynist you are.

CONNOLLY: You've just noticed? (*Beat.*) 'Buttocks' Brownell.

ORWELL: Sorry?

CONNOLLY: Sonia's nickname in the office: 'Buttocks' Brownell. No serious person can have a nickname like 'Buttocks'.

ORWELL: Virginia Woolf used to call you 'The Baboon'.

CONNOLLY: She should have looked in the mirror herself. She had a nose bigger than Swindon; when she drowned it took most of the river to fill her nostrils.

ORWELL: Don't speak ill of the dead. Your reputation for speaking ill of the living is bad enough.

CONNOLLY: *Moi?* I consider myself awash with affection and sweetness.

ORWELL: You are. Until you pick up a pen. (*Beat.*) Why are you here, Cyril?

CONNOLLY: Life gets much more tedious as you get older. There's only the communion of artists keeps us alive.

ORWELL: You've come to commune with me?

CONNOLLY: I spent nearly the whole of the war in London, George.

ORWELL: I know.

CONNOLLY: Saw more death and destruction than I care to mention but do you know something? It was probably the time of my life.

ORWELL: You're missing the Second World War?

CONNOLLY: Peace seems so petty somehow. Keeping *Horizon* going against the onslaught of the barbarians at the gate was the most important thing I've ever done. My life's so irrelevant in comparison now.

ORWELL: The barbarians are still out there, Cyril.

CONNOLLY: I know. And they have the atom bomb. It's closing time in the gardens of the West, George I despair of the civilised world. (*Beat.*) Well, at least until dinner.

ORWELL: What are you getting at, Cyril?

CONNOLLY: You asked me why I've come here.

ORWELL: Yes.

CONNOLLY: I've been your friend since you were nine years old.

ORWELL: So?

CONNOLLY: I've come to stop you making the biggest mistake of your –

At this moment ORWELL starts to cough violently and desperately. He puts a hanky to his mouth. When he removes the hanky it is blood stained.

Dear God, that's blood.

ORWELL: I'm afraid so.

He continues coughing violently. SONIA enters with a pot of tea. She puts it down and crosses to ORWELL.

I do apologise – (*He coughs into the handkerchief again.*)

SONIA: I knew this would happen. You've tired yourself out.

CONNOLLY: He always tires himself out.

SONIA: Working ten to twelve hours a day in these
conditions –

ORWELL: I'm perfectly capable –

ORWELL coughing interrupts his sentence.

SONIA: No, you're not, George. You could have stayed in
London. Who in their right mind would come here?

ORWELL: I get sidetracked by people in London and by
writing articles. Anyway, I like it here.

SONIA: You're downright perverse.

CONNOLLY: He's been the same way since he was small. He's
proved John Donne wrong; one man can indeed be an
island.

SONIA: The damp climate on this island is precisely the
opposite of the high altitude and dry air recommended for
patients with lung disease. He's killing himself.

CONNOLLY: I'd take him back to London in an instant.

ORWELL: I like the isolation.

SONIA: Any mountain you care to climb is just as lonely and
three times as healthy.

ORWELL: I've never been fond of mountains.

SONIA: You've never been fond of anything practical.

ORWELL coughs aggressively into his handkerchief again.

ORWELL: Excuse me.

*ORWELL exits up the stairs. They listen as his wracked coughs
fades.*

37

CONNOLLY: Has he been like this all week?

SONIA: Yes.

CONNOLLY: You should have let someone know.

SONIA: He wouldn't let me.

CONNOLLY: No. (*Beat.*) Even at school he knew no fear.

SONIA: Any rational man should fear dying.

CONNOLLY: Why are you here, Sonia?

SONIA: He invited me.

CONNOLLY: And?

SONIA: And nothing.

She pours him some tea and then adds some Scotch.

CONNOLLY: Still, you look well.

SONIA: Do I? I was up half the night.

CONNOLLY: Naked?

SONIA: In pyjamas, I was reading his novel.

CONNOLLY: You're Julia.

SONIA: I know.

CONNOLLY: Flattered?

SONIA: Not at all.

CONNOLLY: Surely you are, to have an entire book written about you? You: 'the Euston Road Venus'.

SONIA: Back to that?

CONNOLLY: Naturally.

SONIA: How's Lys?

CONNOLLY: Rather fed up. I'm taking it out on her because you're not there to protect me from the literary hordes.

SONIA: It's time you took an interest again. It is your magazine, after all.

CONNOLLY: Not so much mine. (*Mock pompous.*) It belongs to the world.

SONIA: If you say so.

CONNOLLY: What did you think?

SONIA: Of what?

CONNOLLY: The book: naturally.

SONIA: It's brilliant of course.

CONNOLLY: I know. The bastard sent me the first draft.

SONIA: Jealous?

CONNOLLY: Insanely. (*Beat.*) It's always harder when it's a school friend having the success. No matter how supportive you want to be.

SONIA: Did you tell him?

CONNOLLY: What?

SONIA: That you thought it was brilliant?

CONNOLLY: Of course not. (*Beat.*) Slept with him yet?

SONIA: No.

CONNOLLY: Liar.

SONIA: Once.

CONNOLLY: Any good?

SONIA: He seemed pleased.

CONNOLLY: Were you?

SONIA: Not particularly.

CONNOLLY: Excellent.

SONIA: You're that competitive?

CONNOLLY: I'm a man aren't I? (*Beat.*) Speaking of sex –

SONIA: Must you always?

CONNOLLY: While we're here, far from gossiping tongues, any chance – as they say in proletarian circles – of a 'bunk up'?

SONIA: Lys is one of my closest friends.

CONNOLLY: Lys is a thousand miles away.

SONIA: Is that the only reason you came?

CONNOLLY: One of the reasons.

SONIA: You could have any number of literary groupies.

CONNOLLY: They're not you. Why do you sleep with men out of pity?

SONIA: Do I?

CONNOLLY: You know you do, with the exception of the Frenchman. You're an Englishwoman. Why do you prefer to take a Frenchman to bed?

SONIA: I've news for you: most Englishwomen prefer to take a Frenchman to bed.

CONNOLLY: He'll never marry you, of course.

SONIA: That's over.

CONNOLLY: Is it?

SONIA: Completely.

CONNOLLY: So George has a chance?

SONIA: I don't think of him that way.

CONNOLLY: In what way do you think of him?

SONIA: As a friend.

CONNOLLY: And does George see you 'as a friend'?

SONIA: He has a crush on me.

CONNOLLY: Don't we all?

SONIA: If only you didn't. It's so tiresome.

CONNOLLY: You know, I've always considered you my enemy, Sonia, in an unconscious kind of way.

SONIA: Enemy?

CONNOLLY: You're the original Art Tart. You use your good looks to play an important role in literary life. I would never have employed you if you hadn't have been gorgeous.

SONIA: I thought you employed me because I was efficient.

CONNOLLY: That you turned out to be brilliant at your job is neither here not there. But you're the antithesis of sex: a professional virgin, all hockey sticks and repressed lesbianism, a muff-diver in fear of the muff.

SONIA: I'm not a dyke, Cyril.

CONNOLLY: Prove it.

SONIA: Is that all you want from me, Cyril? For me to open my legs and think of England?

CONNOLLY: You can think of any country you like. (*Opens his flies.*) I'm afraid you've left me no choice. I'm going to have to show you this.

CONNOLLY (with his back to the audience please.) reveals his penis.

41

SONIA: I'm sorry, is that your penis or is there a garden worm at large in your trousers?

CONNOLLY: I'm going to seduce you, Sonia.

SONIA: Not by flashing your quite inconsiderable willy you're not.

CONNOLLY: As Flaubert once said 'anything becomes interesting if you look at it long enough'.

SONIA: He never saw your penis.

CONNOLLY: I assure you he would have been fascinated, legions of women are. They either sing hymns of praise or faint when they see it.

SONIA: Why are you doing this, Cyril?

CONNOLLY: If I seduce you then George will fall out of love with you.

SONIA: Why would you want him to do that?

CONNOLLY: Because you'll break his heart.

SONIA: What about my heart?

CONNOLLY: I'm not sure you have one, dear.

SONIA: That's a terrible thing to say.

CONNOLLY: Now's the time to say terrible things: before he comes back.

SONIA: Can you put your penis back in your underwear please? It's making me nauseous or hysterical. I can't quite decide which.

CONNOLLY puts away his penis and does up his fly.

You really are the most extraordinary man.

CONNOLLY: I admit it. I am not a normal person.

SONIA: If only you talked less and wrote more.

CONNOLLY: That's the tragedy of my life. What's yours?

SONIA: What do you think?

CONNOLLY: I think you're essentially talent-less but dream of being talented. Thus you have to be near the gifted and artistic. In case some of it rubs off on you.

SONIA: Funny, I've heard people say the same about you.

CONNOLLY: You see? We're practically twins. Fuck me.

SONIA: Never in a month of Sundays.

CONNOLLY: I do believe you're repulsed by sex, you know.

SONIA: It depends who I'm having the sex with.

CONNOLLY: Says you.

SONIA: Why are you being so protective of George anyway?

CONNOLLY: He knows nothing of women. He never will.

SONIA: And you do, I suppose?

CONNOLLY: I know too much about women. It's been my curse.

SONIA: Go home, Cyril.

CONNOLLY: Not without you. I'm not leaving you here with George.

SONIA: You're being over-protective and silly.

CONNOLLY: Not me. I know a manipulative bitch when I see one. I've been looking at one in the mirror for years.

There is the sound of footsteps on the stairs.

He's coming back. Don't mention the flashing.

SONIA: Why not?

CONNOLLY: He'll think it rude.

ORWELL enters through the door to the stairs, wiping his mouth with a clean hankie.

ORWELL: Sorry about that.

CONNOLLY: Shouldn't you see a doctor?

ORWELL: All I ever see is doctors. Every month I go to Glasgow for a check-up. I've already been in the sanatorium once this year. I need time.

SONIA: The book's nearly finished. You should rest.

ORWELL: When it's finished, another day, perhaps two.

SONIA: You're dead on your feet, man.

CONNOLLY: Don't interrupt a man on a crusade.

ORWELL: Is it a crusade?

CONNOLLY: Of course. Spain's over, George: it proved Hollywood wrong, the good guys lost.

ORWELL: Spain will never be over, Cyril. I owe it to the Spanish dead to finish this book. Our job is to make life worth living.

CONNOLLY: 'What's your proposal, to build the Just City?'

ORWELL: Don't quote Auden at me, Cyril.

CONNOLLY: Why not?

ORWELL: Because he's as self-absorbed as you; it's always the same pattern: you go to public school, then university, take a few trips aboard then move to London to socialise with the same people you went to college with in the first place. And you wonder why you can't write? Why not try starting writing for people instead of your smug bloody social set?

CONNOLLY: Don't turn on me because you're coughing up
blood.

SONIA: Look, stop annoying George. You should get out of
that wet suit anyway. Or you'll catch your death.

CONNOLLY: Finally, she wants to see me naked.

ORWELL: Cyril.

CONNOLLY: Joking, I'm joking.

SONIA: We have blankets upstairs. Come along, Cyril.

CONNOLLY: Yes Julia.

SONIA: Don't call me that. (*To ORWELL.*) Put more wood on
the fire, George. Or we'll all die of cold. We're not all as
Viking as you.

CONNOLLY: They had pigeon-chested Vikings?

SONIA: (*Pushes CONNOLLY up stairs.*) Be quiet, for once in your
life.

*SONIA and CONNOLLY exit up the stairs. CONNOLLY picking up
the bottle of Scotch from the tray as he goes.*

*ORWELL stacks more wood on the fire. PIG appears again, lowering
from the ceiling on a circus swing.*

PIG: Well, getting into her knickers again or what?

ORWELL: Piss off, Stalin. There's a good pig.

PIG: You're so hostile to me, George.

ORWELL: Why wouldn't I be?

PIG: Yet I'm so popular in Bloomsbury.

ORWELL: That's because the English intelligentsia don't
know what socialism is. Why are the English poor so
unimportant to the English Left, because they're not
foreign and faraway? They talk of the 'masses' but can't

45

even see them, every day, all around them. Yet as soon as they see a photo of a bronzed Soviet worker on a tractor ploughing up the Steppes for wheat they're practically erect.

PIG: So they should be.

ORWELL: I was once riding on a train from Wigan and as we got past the station we passed rows and rows of slum housing. At the back of one of them a young woman was poking a stick up a waste pipe, to unblock it I suppose, and she looked up as the train went by. I saw her face for a second. She was twenty-five but looked forty, exhausted and fed up and old before her time. I saw in that girl's face the understanding of how dreadful it was to be kneeling in a slum backyard, poking a stick up a rusting drainpipe. And the automatic assumption by both of us it was her life sentence. That's what socialism should be: the eradication of that destiny. Not about perpetuating a murderous regime that long ago ceased to justify its own existence.

PIG: So a squint-eyed, bandy-legged, working-class bint had to unbung a drain? Boo-hoo. Big bloody deal.

ORWELL: She was a young woman suffering.

PIG: So what? She could always go on the game. Social democracy won't save her.

ORWELL: That's its purpose.

PIG: Bullshit. Governments liberal and conservative come and go. It's still a capitalist economy. The rich get richer, the poor get shafted. Slums, like death and taxes, go on forever.

ORWELL: I disagree. Socialism can solve –

PIG: An old Etonian lecturing me on the merits of socialism? Ha. Stop playing at poverty, George.

ORWELL: My class is dying out. It's about time. We have nothing to lose but our aitches.

PIG: And an Empire don't forget. An Empire you served; an Empire that's murdered half the world.

ORWELL: How is it only the British murder people? In the Soviet Union they get 'liquidated'. What's the matter? Scared of saying the word? Murder is murder in any language.

PIG: Change the record, George.

ORWELL: You've slaughtered just about every significant writer in Russia. If not by the bullet then by the Gulag –

PIG: You're getting paranoid, George. Why would I be bothered about killing writers, the most inept, pissed, and whining members of any society?

ORWELL: They'll bring you down yet.

PIG: Nuclear weapons will bring me down, George, and I fall I take the world with me. Now your cheery Eton-educated traitors have given me access to the bomb. You can't kill anything with just a pen, let alone a dictator. Spit in a dole queue you'll hit a thousand writers. Face it, you bastards are expendable.

ORWELL: You're a swine.

PIG: You've noticed.

ORWELL: But I've seen to your lackeys in this country, don't you worry. I've composed a list of every death camp apologist and crypto-communist I can think of, over a hundred names. I've sent it to the Attlee administration.

PIG: But George, that's squealing.

ORWELL: If 'squealing' keeps the West free then so be it.

PIG: But condemning people with lists is what I do. Turning into me, George?

ORWELL: You fight fire with fire. That's why if you send your NKVD goons my shotgun is ready and waiting.

PIG: Why not use the gun for why you've really bought it? To blow your stupid, melancholy brains out.

ORWELL: Why on earth would I do that?

PIG: Because I've won George; I won in Spain. Now I have Eastern Europe by the balls. Your People's War didn't save them. It didn't save anyone. Capitalism was not vanquished. Only its bastard offspring – fascism. Your dream is over, George. It never had a chance. People are selfish scum, end of story. Pick up the shotgun, aim it at the old noggin, be miserable no more; time to bite the proverbial bullet, you know it makes sense.

ORWELL: Get out of here, you little bastard, and right now.

PIG: What will you do if I don't? Write another reactionary fucking book?

ORWELL: I've shot at fascists I can shoot at swine; there's little difference save the bloody uniform.

PIG: I'll be back.

ORWELL: I wouldn't count on it.

PIG: Menshevik.

PIG disappears into the ceiling on his rope swing. A silence then footsteps are heard on the stairs. SONIA enters from the doorway to the stairs.

ORWELL: Where's Cyril?

SONIA: Taking his clothes off.

ORWELL: I'd rather not picture that.

SONIA: He was quite keen for me to join him.

ORWELL: Did he tell you why he was here?

SONIA: Not really.

ORWELL: You'd think *Horizon* would need him, you being away.

SONIA: It does. We're desperately short of subscribers and the income tax people are on our backs constantly. The whole thing seems to be collapsing like a deck of cards. It's such a bloody shame.

ORWELL: What will you do if it folds?

SONIA: I don't know. It's been my life for years.

ORWELL: There are other editing jobs, surely.

SONIA: Perhaps, I'm not going back to typing, I know that much. Anything to avoid the normal life; I just don't want to end up back in South Ken, a dreary housewife.

ORWELL: I can't imagine you being dreary in any capacity.

SONIA: You'd be surprised. I can be as dull as the best of them.

ORWELL: Not you. You look like someone painted by Renoir.

SONIA: It's not all it's made out to be, being beautiful, George.

ORWELL: I wouldn't know.

SONIA: Most men hate you for it somewhere along the line. You're never quite sure if you're being taken seriously.

ORWELL: I take you seriously, Sonia.

SONIA: Do you?

ORWELL: Oh yes.

SONIA: When I was at my convent school I used to lie awake at night dreaming of escape. I wanted to do something wonderful, something amazing with my life. I didn't know what. I just knew it had to be something extraordinary. Well, I found the artistic life but not the gifts to go with it. I'll never write a novel, never be a poet, never be a painter; I'll do nothing.

ORWELL: You inspire a lot of us, me anyway.

SONIA: Cyril thinks I'm a literary groupie. He calls me the 'Art Tart'.

ORWELL: Cyril's living proof men only give their penis's names because they don't want their lives run by a stranger.

SONIA: Is that all I am to you, a literary groupie?

ORWELL: No, you're Julia.

SONIA: I wish you hadn't written about me like that.

ORWELL: I had to. I'm infatuated with you.

SONIA: I won't sleep with you again, George.

ORWELL: Didn't you enjoy it?

SONIA: Not much.

ORWELL: Might I ask why?

SONIA: It had a touch of the brothel about it: wham, bam and thank you, Ma'am.

ORWELL: I got rather used to brothels in Burma; there were no white women for hundreds of miles you see. It probably taught me bad habits –

SONIA: Too much information, George.

ORWELL: – But last night wasn't just sex to me, you know.

SONIA: I told you it was just some fun.

ORWELL: I don't treat you that lightly.

SONIA: Why ever not? Most people do.

ORWELL: You're too important to me.

SONIA: Oh God.

ORWELL: Couldn't we try again?

SONIA: I don't think so.

ORWELL: It might get better.

SONIA: It's not about technique.

ORWELL: Please?

SONIA: Don't George –

ORWELL: I know I'm not much to look at but –

SONIA: Please stop, George.

ORWELL: Just one more night.

SONIA: You're so desperate.

ORWELL: I have no pride where you're concerned.

SONIA: I've noticed.

ORWELL: I need you.

SONIA: George, please. Don't say these things.

ORWELL: I'd do anything –

SONIA: I've said no.

ORWELL: Please –

SONIA: (*Louder.*) No.

> *There is terrible, awkward silence. ORWELL looks close to desperate tears. At this moment RAT enters from the kitchen. He is a six-foot rodent, wearing a kilt and smoking a cigar, genial of disposition; obviously SONIA cannot see a figment of ORWELL's imagination.*

ORWELL: Did I mention the rat?

SONIA: (*Worried.*) There's a rat?

RAT: I hate to interrupt this beautiful moment but might this be the way to Room 101?

ORWELL stares at the RAT. The RAT stares back. SONIA looks confused. A distant grandfather clock chimes thirteen times rapidly as the lights fade to black.

Act Two

Music: An instrumental version of 'Love for Sale'.

The same as Act One; it is now three o'clock the next morning. The room is lit by storm-lanterns which give the room an ethereal, dream-like quality.

The music fades.

ORWELL sits at his typewriter alone, furiously typing. He stops typing abruptly and stares at the page.

Enter RAT – in his kilt – through the door to the kitchen. He smokes his cigar; he is the benign, friendly type.

RAT: Evening George.

ORWELL: Hello Rat, what kept you?

RAT: I'm afraid I had to rifle your cupboards for food.

ORWELL: Find any?

RAT: Not a thing. I know rationing is the order of the day but you should really stock up more.

ORWELL: I believe there's some porridge.

RAT: Even rodents turn their noses up at glorified gruel.

ORWELL: It'll put hairs on your chest.

RAT: I'm a rat. I already have hairs on my chest.

ORWELL: But of course.

RAT glances around him.

RAT: Is this your Room 101, George, it seems so to me.

ORWELL: It's not so bad.

RAT: Isn't it? The war's over. Why not go back to London? Why suffer any more? You've done your bit for the Common Man.

ORWELL: I'm not particularly fond of London, Rat. Or people.

RAT: I like London. There's two rats for every Londoner. They carry diseases and have terrible hygiene but the rats just hold their noses and ignore them.

RAT laughs.

ORWELL: Very good.

RAT: So what are you writing?

ORWELL: The last pages.

RAT picks up the front page of the manuscript on the table.

RAT: Ah, our manuscript. Why 1984 of all years?

ORWELL: Can't you guess?

RAT: Not off-hand.

ORWELL: It's a Year of the Rat, like this one.

RAT: Every year is a Year of the Rat in my world, George. In your next book can we have more positive rodent characters please?

ORWELL: I don't know if I have the energy for another book, Rat. I hope otherwise. But hope has a way of punching you in the mouth.

RAT: What's the future hold for you, George?

ORWELL: I – can't say.

RAT: But is this all there is for you, just this, lighthouse days, social isolation, book after book, the eternal typist?

ORWELL: It seems so.

RAT: Why the inertia? You know what has to be done. You must change the situation, take the bull by the horns, go in like Flynn; after all, faint heart never won fair lady.

ORWELL: Have you entered a meaningless cliché competition without telling me, Rat?

RAT: You know what I mean.

ORWELL: Yes.

RAT: Will you ask her?

ORWELL: Perhaps.

RAT: There's no perhaps about it. You must ask her, without me as an excuse. You've already left it too long.

ORWELL: I thought I had the week, until Cyril came.

RAT: Are you worthy of her?

ORWELL: Probably not.

RAT: Self-loathing is a terrible thing, George. It's the enemy within. The rest of the world queues up to drag you down. Why join them?

ORWELL: Do you think I'm foolish?

RAT: I can't advise you on affairs of the heart. Rats don't have feelings. We just stuff our faces and have endless sex.

ORWELL: You should meet Cyril.

RAT: Time for love, old son; time to come in from the cold; time to abandon Sparta.

ORWELL: If I were from Sparta my parents would have left me outside to die. They did that with the sick runts of the litter.

RAT: This isn't Sparta, George, just your artificial version of it. You've spent your life preaching humanity for the world. Perhaps that's failed but you can at least release

55

the humanity in yourself. Your marriage was emotionally frigid. You know that. Time to lower the drawbridge to your heart – it's been closed too long.

ORWELL: Are you my fear, Rat?

RAT: Of course I am, old son. Just as our friend the pig is your hopelessness; we all have our role in this.

ORWELL: Fear of what?

RAT: Dying alone, dying with your dreams defeated. What else?

ORWELL: I see.

RAT: Prove us both wrong, George. Love someone.

ORWELL: But why would someone love me, Rat?

RAT: Why not? You're only as ugly as the next human. (*Winks.*) Now a scantily-clad hamster, that's a different story.

There are footsteps on the stairs. RAT moves towards the door to the kitchen.

I'd better disappear. Good luck, George.

ORWELL: I'm not sure I have that.

RAT: Then courage, sir.

ORWELL: I'm not I have that either.

RAT exits back into the kitchen. A long beat then CONNOLLY enters through the doorway to the stairs. He is wrapped in blankets, wearing only his trousers and a vest beneath. He carries a bottle of Scotch, mostly drunk.

CONNOLLY: I heard voices.

ORWELL: It was just me.

CONNOLLY: It's the first sign of madness.

ORWELL: What is?

CONNOLLY: Talking to yourself.

ORWELL: I wasn't.

CONNOLLY: Who were you talking to?

ORWELL: A rat.

CONNOLLY: You talk to rats?

ORWELL: Sometimes they even talk back.

CONNOLLY: Not still here is it?

ORWELL: No, you'd notice it. Trust me.

CONNOLLY: What a God-awful place this is. Still, at least it gets you away from the English. We're a terrible people: sheep who can turn nasty.

ORWELL: Couldn't sleep?

CONNOLLY: I'm afraid I had to partake of your last bottle of Scotch.

ORWELL: It's the one thing easily purchased on this island.

CONNOLLY: I've been thinking.

ORWELL: About what?

CONNOLLY: You actually.

ORWELL: I'm flattered.

CONNOLLY: You shouldn't be. Do you know I've never seen you in an overcoat?

ORWELL: No?

CONNOLLY: Never seen a photo of you in one either. Not in all these years.

ORWELL: Really?

CONNOLLY: What kind of man doesn't wear an overcoat?

ORWELL: Me apparently.

CONNOLLY: You just wear those God-awful tweed jackets.

ORWELL: I've always thought of myself as sartorially elegant.

CONNOLLY: You dress like a farmer, George.

ORWELL: Thank you.

CONNOLLY: It kept me awake, the thought. You've always been unwell and yet you've never worn an overcoat. Why is that?

ORWELL: I'm pretty robust.

CONNOLLY: Despite all evidence to the contrary.

ORWELL: I've always despised hypochondria.

CONNOLLY: I've always warmly embraced it, like a personal friend. I take to my bed at the first sniffle, gargling brandy like Nero after an orgy. Which is why I've always been physically in the pink and you're such a walking ghoul.

ORWELL: Not a ghoul yet.

CONNOLLY: Soon – if you continue on your voyage of self-destruction.

ORWELL: I'm not on a voyage of self-destruction.

CONNOLLY: You're fooling no one. (*Beat.*) Come back to London.

ORWELL: I can't.

CONNOLLY: Won't more like.

ORWELL: Won't then.

CONNOLLY: You're a success. Don't you want to revel in it?

ORWELL: Not in the least.

CONNOLLY: I would. But why torment myself? I'll never write a great book. I know that now.

ORWELL: Don't say that.

CONNOLLY: It's the truth. The question I have to ask is – why you? Why not me?

ORWELL: I can't answer that.

CONNOLLY: The muse will never be upon me. You seem to fuck it on a whim.

ORWELL: You can have sexual intercourse with a muse?

CONNOLLY: You shag the bitch gleefully. But to me her legs are forever closed.

ORWELL: I do believe you're drunk, Cyril.

CONNOLLY: I do believe I am. Yes, I do believe I am. (*Beat.*) Sonia drinks of course.

ORWELL: Does she?

CONNOLLY: Like a fish, drinks so much gin Hogarth painted her. She's sloshed most nights in Soho; has handles on her knickers so they can carry her to the cab quicker when she passes out.

ORWELL: Why do you keep putting her down?

CONNOLLY: Because I have to; she's still in love with the Frenchman. Did you know?

ORWELL: The Frenchman?

CONNOLLY: Sartre and de Beauvoir's crony, old twinkle-toes; who'd have thought an existentialist could do the foxtrot? Or would want to?

ORWELL: Who are you talking about?

CONNOLLY: The philosopher: Merleau-Ponty. He cuts quite a rug.

ORWELL: How do you know she's still in love with him?

CONNOLLY: You can see it in her eyes. Though she says it's over.

ORWELL: Well, that's good.

CONNOLLY: No, it's not. (*Beat.*) I've asked her to come back with me.

ORWELL: When?

CONNOLLY: In the morning, the office has gone to pot without her.

ORWELL: What did she say?

CONNOLLY: She's said she'll come. Frankly I don't think she's comfortable here.

ORWELL: Why not?

CONNOLLY: You keep gazing at her like a lovesick gazelle is why not.

ORWELL: I can't tell you the harm you're doing here. You should never have come.

CONNOLLY: She's been here three days.

ORWELL: What about it?

CONNOLLY: You can discuss the history of the world in three days and still have time for tea. What else do you possibly have to talk about?

ORWELL: Things.

CONNOLLY: Too late.

ORWELL: You selfish bastard.

CONNOLLY: Charming.

ORWELL: If you were my friend you'd leave.

CONNOLLY: I'm being a better friend than you'll ever know.

ORWELL: You're only here because you want Sonia.

CONNOLLY: I admit there's an element of sexual jealousy.
Nothing stirs a man's lusts quite like the pursuit of the
unobtainable. But my intentions are honourable this time. I
got your manuscript.

ORWELL: What was the wrong with my manuscript?

CONNOLLY: Nothing was wrong with it, quite the opposite.
I envy you the smallest fart of your talent. It scared the
bloody life out of me it was that good. It was the letter that
came with it brought me here.

*CONNOLLY goes to behind the door, parts the coats and brings out
the shotgun hiding there.*

You told me you'd brought this.

ORWELL: And?

CONNOLLY: I put two and two together –

ORWELL: And made five; I'm not going to do anything rash.
I bought the gun to shoot game and any of Stalin's goons
that come for me.

CONNOLLY: Are you telling me you brought this gun to shoot
rabbits and/or Russians?

ORWELL: Yes.

CONNOLLY: Well, I'm relieved, more than relieved.

ORWELL: How do you mean?

CONNOLLY: I presumed you'd purchased it to blow your
brains out. In fact I was sure of it.

ORWELL: You really must spend more time in the country, Cyril, we use guns for other things than blowing our brains out.

CONNOLLY: But what are you going to do when Sonia rejects you?

ORWELL: She's not going to reject me.

CONNOLLY: Of course she's going to reject you.

ORWELL: (*Shouts.*) How do you know?

CONNOLLY: (*Shouts.*) Because it's bloody obvious.

ORWELL: (*Shouts.*) Why is it bloody obvious?

CONNOLLY: (*Shouts.*) Because she's gorgeous and you're a bloody scarecrow.

ORWELL: (*Shouts.*) Better than being a bloated bloody gargoyle like you.

CONNOLLY: (*Shouts.*) This gargoyle has fucked more women than the Grenadier fucking Guards.

ORWELL: Stop interfering.

CONNOLLY: Is there no one else? There must be someone else.

ORWELL: No, there's not, she's my last chance saloon.

CONNOLLY: Then God pity you.

ORWELL: I've never believed in the fellow upstairs, you know that. Heaven and hell, it's here on earth, we make of it what we will.

CONNOLLY: Pity yourself then.

ORWELL: I do, too much.

SONIA enters from the doorway to the stairs.

SONIA: I heard shouting.

CONNOLLY: That's because there was shouting.

SONIA: What are you doing up, George? I thought I'd put you to bed.

ORWELL: I couldn't sleep.

SONIA: You were writing, weren't you?

ORWELL: What have you been saying to Cyril?

SONIA: He wasn't supposed to say anything.

ORWELL: Well, I'm afraid he did.

SONIA: I was going to tell you in the morning.

ORWELL: Tell me what?

SONIA: I'm going back to London, first thing.

ORWELL: But you promised to stay for a week.

SONIA: I can't bear to see you like this.

ORWELL: I'll be worse without you.

SONIA: I can't be responsible for you, George.

ORWELL: I don't want you to be.

SONIA: But you're asking too much.

ORWELL: I always ask too much. Of myself and others; I know no other way.

SONIA: We can't all be as pure as you.

ORWELL: Why not?

CONNOLLY: Let's all go to bed. We can discuss this in the cold light of day.

SONIA: Don't sound reasonable now, Cyril. You've done enough harm.

CONNOLLY: Harm in a good cause.

SONIA: I asked you not to say anything.

CONNOLLY: He's my friend.

SONIA: And I'm not?

CONNOLLY: You're a woman first.

SONIA: I could hit you sometimes.

CONNOLLY: Join the queue.

SONIA: You blunder in –

CONNOLLY: Where angels fear to tread.

SONIA: You're no bloody angel.

CONNOLLY: No, but it's all about trying.

ORWELL: Cyril, would you mind leaving us?

CONNOLLY: I'm afraid I can't do that.

ORWELL: Why not?

CONNOLLY: You know why not.

ORWELL: You've said your piece.

CONNOLLY: I haven't even begun.

ORWELL: Please go upstairs.

CONNOLLY: George, you'll have your heart broken in –

ORWELL: Go. Please.

CONNOLLY: I refuse to let this –

ORWELL: Cyril.

CONNOLLY: Very well, I've tried my best.

CONNOLLY exits unwillingly up the stairs. An awkward silence.

SONIA: What on earth has got into him?

ORWELL: My Scotch mostly, he wanted to stop me talking to you.

SONIA: George, I won't have sex with you again.

ORWELL: It's not about that.

SONIA: It's not?

ORWELL: It's about something altogether more serious.

SONIA: I've no idea what you're getting at.

ORWELL: Don't you?

SONIA: Not in the least. You're talking in riddles.

ORWELL: I know I wouldn't be your ideal choice.

SONIA: Of what, George? Please come to the point.

ORWELL: I know this will come as something as a shock –

SONIA: Do come out with it, George.

ORWELL: Would you consider marrying me?

SONIA: What?

ORWELL: I want you to marry me, Sonia.

SONIA: If I'd know that I would never have come here.

ORWELL: But you did. Might you?

SONIA: You hardly know me.

ORWELL: I know you well enough.

SONIA: You've had sex with me, there's a difference.

ORWELL: Is there someone else?

SONIA: There was but that doesn't matter now.

ORWELL: The Frenchman?

SONIA: Yes.

ORWELL: Did you love him?

SONIA: Yes.

ORWELL: Did he love you?

SONIA: Yes.

ORWELL: But doesn't now?

SONIA: He wanted a mistress, I wanted a husband.

ORWELL: What did you see in him?

SONIA: Everything.

ORWELL: Be specific.

SONIA: Must I?

ORWELL: You must.

SONIA: You see, he danced.

ORWELL: I'm sorry?

SONIA: He's the only intellectual I knew ever danced, save for Cyril. Why is it none of you dance?

ORWELL: I don't know.

SONIA: There's something wonderful about forgetting yourself in music.

ORWELL: I don't suppose I'm fit enough to dance, not these days.

SONIA: Did you ever?

ORWELL: No, I can't say I did.

SONIA: Why not?

ORWELL: Is it important?

SONIA: It is to me.

ORWELL: I expect I thought it was frivolous.

SONIA: I expect you did. We'd never dance, George, would we?

ORWELL: No.

SONIA: You see?

ORWELL: It's no reason not to marry someone.

SONIA: It's one of a hundred. Why do you need me, George?

ORWELL: I need someone to care about me.

SONIA: Of course I care about you.

ORWELL: Well then? I know I'm not much cop physically –

SONIA: Please, don't go on.

ORWELL: We wouldn't be married for long. I've got a couple of years left at the most. You'd be the widow of a literary man.

SONIA: But why would I want that?

ORWELL: *Animal Farm* is ridiculously successful. This is your chance to be financially independent. Isn't that something you've always dreamed of?

SONIA: You make it sound like a business deal.

ORWELL: It is. I need someone to look after my affairs, protect my work, make sure the boy gets his inheritance; you could re-marry, after I've gone.

SONIA: I can't marry you. I'm fond of you, really fond of you, and I want the best for you but I believe in love.

ORWELL: So do I.

SONIA: Entering into a literary 'arrangement' isn't my idea of love. I need love too. (*Beat.*) I'm as lonely as you.

ORWELL: So we could be lonely together.

SONIA: Faking it, just for the sake of it? I couldn't live that way. I don't think you could either.

ORWELL: Stay, a few days longer. We can talk more.

SONIA: Cyril needs me. The office has gone to hell.

ORWELL: I'd come to London if you married me.

SONIA: That's just emotional blackmail.

ORWELL: I know it.

SONIA: It's beneath you.

ORWELL: Nothing's beneath me where you're concerned. I'd give up this place without a second's hesitation. As you've asked, it's what you want isn't it?

SONIA: I just can't, George.

ORWELL: You might change your mind.

SONIA: I'll never change my mind.

ORWELL stares at her, defeated.

ORWELL: I thought it was a woman's privilege.

SONIA: Not this woman's.

A bitter silence.

ORWELL: You realise I'll ask again.

SONIA: Please don't.

ORWELL: If only I were handsome.

SONIA: Why torment yourself?

ORWELL: Because I can.

SONIA: Come with us in the morning.

ORWELL: My life is here.

SONIA: What life? The book's finished. You'd be closer to a sanatorium –

ORWELL: My health is of no consequence to me whatsoever.

SONIA: But it has to be, if you're to go on.

ORWELL: Who said I was going on?

SONIA: I'm begging you.

ORWELL: I belong here.

SONIA: There's nothing for you here.

ORWELL: There's solitude. I was hoping you might want to share it but I was mistaken.

SONIA: But for God's sakes, George –

ORWELL: You'd better go to bed now.

SONIA: George –

ORWELL: Please, go.

SONIA walks to the doorway leading to the stairs; turns.

SONIA: Will I see you in the morning?

ORWELL: Why wouldn't you?

SONIA: I'm – sorry.

ORWELL: Everyone's sorry: it's an English disease.

With a hopeless last look SONIA exits up the stairs, a long silence. ORWELL looks on the verge of tears, defeated. He runs his hands over his face. Finally he composes himself. A long beat then BOXER pokes his head through the open window.

BOXER: Are you alright, George?

ORWELL: Not really, Boxer.

BOXER: You look so sad.

ORWELL: I am sad.

BOXER: Why?

ORWELL: It's a terrible long walk from the cradle to the grave when you walk alone, Boxer.

BOXER: You have us, George. The animals love you.

ORWELL: I'm afraid imaginary creatures aren't quite the companionship I was looking for, Boxer. I've relied on you all for too long. It was unfair of me. Sleep now. Sleep forever.

BOXER: But what will you do without us?

ORWELL: I expect I'll manage, somehow.

BOXER: But what if you can't?

ORWELL: Then I face the consequences.

BOXER: You're awfully hard on yourself, George.

ORWELL: I have to be, now more so than ever. Feelings: 'they shall not pass'.

BOXER: They said that at Madrid. And still the fascists came.

ORWELL: I know, Boxer. We must all live with the disappointment of our hopes and dreams. Only God knows how. (*A bleak laugh.*) I keep forgetting.

BOXER: What's that?

ORWELL: I don't believe in God anymore. My faith is social justice. It's a fine thing to believe in but it brings you little comfort at three o'clock in the morning.

BOXER: I don't want to go, George. I don't want to leave you.

ORWELL: You have to, Boxer. I insist upon it. Goodbye now. Remember: four legs are good. It's the two-legged animals who always bring you down.

BOXER: I'll remember, George. I'll remember.

BOXER exits through the window. ORWELL goes to the front door, opens it, picks up the shotgun, steps out of the door, fires both barrels into the night sky, returns through the door and places the shotgun once more behind the door. He staggers slightly from the exertion as he comes back into the room, holding onto a chair and coughing a pained cough several times. The fit passes and he sits.

Footsteps are heard. CONNOLLY re-enters hurriedly through the door to the stairs.

CONNOLLY: Thank God, you're still with us.

ORWELL sits silent.

What were you shooting at?

ORWELL: The future.

CONNOLLY: I don't understand.

ORWELL: No.

CONNOLLY: What's happened?

ORWELL: She's turned me down.

CONNOLLY: I see.

ORWELL: Feel free to say 'I told you so'.

CONNOLLY: Not this time.

ORWELL: It's the end of things.

CONNOLLY: You have books left in you, George. You told me so.

ORWELL: No, I'm all through now, a busted flush.

CONNOLLY: You write to live.

ORWELL: I wrote to live. I'm finished.

CONNOLLY: There's other women.

ORWELL: Sometimes I think you don't know me at all.

A silence, then:

I never loved Eileen. Not really. Lord knows I respected her and liked her but I didn't love her. This was my chance, my one chance. I've done enough to hope for some happiness.

CONNOLLY: It's not too late, man.

ORWELL: Yes it is. Who am I fooling? I've always been a walking corpse. I can't remember a time or a place when I wasn't ill. I was eighteen months old when I first started showing the symptoms. What was it you wrote? 'We are all serving a life sentence in the dungeon of self.' Well, this scarecrow body's my prison; an over-active mind trapped inside an emaciated skeleton, screaming for help from his rotting cell. And like a foolish housewife or the silliest young girl I thought love could free me. There's no fool like a dying fool.

A silence, then:

CONNOLLY: I thought if I could seduce Sonia you'd hate her, George. And be free. When that didn't work I thought if I got her back to London you'd follow. I didn't realise the extent of things. I'm sorry.

ORWELL: Why would you do all that, Cyril?

CONNOLLY: You're my oldest friend. I don't want you to die here.

ORWELL: The first word I ever said was 'beastly' apparently, according to my mother. I've found existence pretty beastly since. Dying would be a rest from that, wouldn't it, a wonderful rest. It's been such a bloody life, Cyril, such a bloody life.

CONNOLLY: For what it's worth I think you're the most honest writer of your generation and probably the conscience of it.

ORWELL: For what it's worth. (*A long beat.*) Do you know something? It's ridiculous, ironic, pathetic I know, but I'd have given it all up, all the success, all the novels, all the praise, just to have been good with girls.

CONNOLLY: I don't know what else to say.

ORWELL: No.

CONNOLLY: You're a good man, George.

ORWELL: I live in a world where nobody cares about that.

CONNOLLY: We have to care about that.

ORWELL: I wish I could share your optimism. Unfortunately optimism is a luxury I can no longer – (*He begins to cough violently.*) – afford.

CONNOLLY: You should go to bed, George. You're not well.

ORWELL: Yes, doctors keep telling me, until I'm literally sick of it.

CONNOLLY: Please, for my sake.

ORWELL: No, I'll watch the fire for a little while. You go up.

CONNOLLY: But George –

ORWELL: It'll be alright, Cyril.

CONNOLLY: Yes. There's always the morning.

ORWELL: Is there?

The RAT enters and watched from the kitchen doorway. As CONNOLLY reaches the stairs he stops, turns and quotes:

CONNOLLY: 'Perhaps one day even these things will be pleasant to remember.'

CONNOLLY exits. ORWELL stares after him then goes to the fire and stares dejectedly into it.

The RAT glances at ORWELL then addresses the audience:

RAT: It was the motto, of their dreaded prep school. But these things are never pleasant to remember. Orwell's lungs finally did for him of course. He was forty-six when finally forced off the island by his health. By the time he'd achieved success he was doomed and knew it. Thus he tasted the bitterness of dying.

The lights change, giving the stage a more ethereal feel. Enter SONIA, now dressed in the fashion of early 1950, the year of ORWELL's death. She begins to tidy his desk.

She married him in the end. He was on his deathbed. She did the decent thing. They were married for a hundred days. He left her rich, a 'Merry Widow', though she seemed to loose everything by the end; she never found the love she was looking for. Who does?

SONIA stares at ORWELL.

SONIA: You said you'd get better if I married you.

ORWELL: I was lying.

SONIA: I know.

ORWELL: You said you'd learn to make dumplings.

SONIA: I was lying too.

ORWELL: We never made the mountains in Switzerland.

SONIA: The sanatorium in the Alps: a fool's dream.

ORWELL: As I lay dying I dreamt of a city by the sea and streets of blinding sunshine and vast, splendid buildings rising into the sky. Passing close to the shore were ships as tall as the sun, gliding past – silent but sure, their sails as white as snow. There were no guns on those ships, for there was no need of guns in that place. I often lost my way in the streets of that city. But I knew I was safe. That I would always be safe there; I knew even then it was a dream of death but I would wake up with a peculiar feeling of happiness and sunshine. And you know what I used to see the moment I woke up?

SONIA: No.

ORWELL: You, asleep in a hospital chair, the morning sun catching the light in your hair, and despite the fact I was dying I felt the luckiest man alive.

SONIA: I wish I could have done more for you George.

ORWELL: What more could you have done?

SONIA: Loved you.

ORWELL: The human heart is not guided by wishful thinking.

SONIA: But that it was, but that it was.

A silence; they stare.

ORWELL: We'll always have that night on Jura.

SONIA: Yes, until better days, George.

ORWELL: Yes, better days.

SONIA exits. ORWELL stares down at the fire once more. The RAT resumes his monologue to the audience.

75

RAT: *Nineteen Eighty-Four* made Orwell the most internationally famous English author of the 20th Century. Cyril Connolly remained a genius without a career; fatally weakened by sloth, self-pity and an inordinate taste for luxury; popping up in the diaries of the more famous and more celebrated. A fat chorus on his times: witty, entertaining but ultimately – pointless. His Room 101, the door marked 'Failure' at the end of the corridor. We all face Room 101 in the end, all of us, even you. The rat in the cage is waiting. And it knows your name.

ORWELL glances up from the fire.

ORWELL: Well?

RAT: Well?

ORWELL: Have you concluded?

RAT: I have.

ORWELL: A decent enough epitaph.

RAT: Free of cant – if not envy.

ORWELL: What more can a man ask?

RAT: What more indeed?

ORWELL: I was almost moved myself.

RAT: Did you build the Just City do you think?

ORWELL: Let posterity be the judge of that.

RAT: Some call you a saint.

ORWELL: A saint, no, I was never the equal of my work. I tried my best. You can only try your best. It's all there is.

RAT: Would she have been happier, if she'd never met you, if she'd never had to carry the torch?

ORWELL: The answer to that, Rat, is written on the wind.

RAT: True.

ORWELL: So, are we done?

RAT: Yes, all done.

ORWELL: Then I have only one question.

RAT: Which is?

ORWELL: Would you like to dance?

RAT: I thought you never danced.

ORWELL: Perhaps it's long time I tried.

RAT: Frankly I thought you'd never ask.

Music begins: an orchestral version of 'Poor Little Rich Girl.' ORWELL begins to dance around the room with RAT, doing an inept if energetic fox trot.

You dance like a Frenchman.

ORWELL: You eat like one.

They dance on. As they do the lights gradually fade to black; the music fades slowly, until there is darkness and silence.

The End.